SURVEY OF LAW SCHOOL FACULTY: POST PANDEMIC PLANS FOR ONLINE INSTRUCTION

 ISBN 978-157440-677-1

Table of Contents

THE QUESTIONNAIRE

1. Please give us the following contact information:

   A. Name:
   B. Organization:
   C. Title
   D. Email Address:

2. You are:

   A. Professor
   B. Assistant/Associate Professor
   C. Lecturer or Research Fellow
   D. Adjunct/Clinical Faculty
   E. Emeritus
   F. Other (please specify)

3. How old are you

   A. Under 35
   B. 35-44
   C. 45-54
   D. 55-65
   E. Over 65

4. Are you male or female?

   A. Male
   B. Female

5. Your law school has approximately how many students?

6. Is your law school public or private?

   A. Public
   B. Private

7. In the past semester how many courses did you teach?

   A. None
   B. One
   C. Two
   D. More than Two

8. Have you used Zoom in any of your courses over the past year?

   A. Yes in all of them
   B. Yes in some of them
   C. No

9. About how many times in the following periods have you sought the assistance of or otherwise interacted with a member of the Information Technology Staff at your law school, either in person or by phone, Skype, Zoom, email or other means?

   A. Year Prior to the Pandemic Ending March 1 2020
   B. March 2020 to March 2021 (During Pandemic)

10. If you taught a course online during the pandemic, how much time in total hours did it take you to prepare this course the first time that you taught it?

11. If you taught or soon will teach this predominantly or completely online course a second time, how much time in hours did it or will it take for you to prepare it?

12. In your online classes how easy is it to integrate course content into your course management system or other online system used to serve your students?

    A. Very easy
    B. Easy
    C. Neither easy nor difficult
    D. Difficult
    E. Very difficult

13. Have you integrated information available at your academic library into the course management system or other online system for your students?

    A. Yes
    B. No
    C. No but I would like to

14. What is the educational quality of the online courses that you have taught relative to in-person courses?

    A. Much better
    B. Better
    C. About the same
    D. Worse
    E. Much worse

15. Post pandemic what percentage of courses that you teach would you like to teach predominantly online?

16. How would you characterize your law school's plans for post pandemic online teaching?

    A. Eliminate online as much as possible
    B. Generally go back to our pre-pandemic practices
    C. Not as much as now but more than before
    D. Much more than before
    E. Not really sure

17. To what extent do you feel that your law school should use online education post pandemic?

   A. Less than before the pandemic
   B. About as much as before the pandemic
   C. More than before the pandemic
   D. Much more than before the pandemic

18. Which law school courses are most and least amenable to online teaching?

19. What new programs or courses do you think the law school has or may now be able to develop now that faculty is more familiar with distance education?

20. What percentage of law school classes do you feel should remain predominantly online post pandemic?

21. What practices that developed during the pandemic do you feel should be held over and extended post pandemic?

INSTITUTIONAL AFFILIATIONS OF THE SUVEY PARTICIPANTS

American University Law School
BGR
Blewett School of Law, University of Montana
Boston College Law School
Boston University School of Law
BU Law School
BYU Law School
Case Western Reserve University
Chicago-Kent College of Law
Columbia Law School
CWRU School of Law
Delaware Law School
Duke School of Law
Florida International University College of Law
George Mason University School of Law (Antonin Scalia Law School)
Georgetown University
IIT Chicago-Kent College of Law
Liberty University School of Law
LMU Loyola Law School Los Angeles
Mercer Law
Mississippi College School of Law
Northern California Innocence Project
Notre Dame Law School
NYU Law School
Pepperdine University Cardozo School of Law
Rutgers University Law School
Santa Clara University
Seton Hall Law School
The University of Alabama School of Law
UC Davis School of Law
University of Akron
University of Connecticut School of Law
University of Florida
University of Florida Legal Information Center
University of Louisville Brandeis School of Law
University of Miami
University of Minnesota Law School
University of Missouri–Kansas City School of Law
University of North Dakota School of Law
University of Oklahoma College of Law
University of Oregon School of Law
University of Pennsylvania Carey Law School
University of Pittsburgh
University of Pittsburgh School of Law
University of San Diego School of Law

USC Gould School of Law
UT School of Law
Villanova School of Law
Washington and Lee Univ. School of Law
Widener University Delaware Law School
William S. Boyd School of Law at University of Nevada

Characteristics of the Sample

Law school ranking

	#
Top 20	20
21-45	30
46-80	30
More than 80	29
Total	109

Title of respondent

	#
Professor	49
Assistant/Associate Professor/Lecturer or Research Fellow	11
Adjunct/Clinical Faculty	38
Emeritus	5
Other	6
Total	109

Age of respondent

	#
44 or under	10
45-54	28
55-65	37
Over 65	34
Total	109

Gender of respondent

	#
Male	77
Female	32
Total	109

Law school student enrollment

	#
Less than 400	23
400 - 500	29
501 - 750	25
More than 750	32
Total	109

Public or private status

	#
Public	46
Private	63
Total	109

Number of courses taught in the past semester

	#
None	9
One	50
Two	38
More than Two	12
Total	109

Summary of Main Findings

Use of Zoom in Law School Classes

We asked: Have you used Zoom in any of your courses over the past year?

A large majority of 80.73% used Zoom in all of their courses over the past year and 4,59% in just some of them. At the lowest ranked schools, only 62.1% of faculty had used Zoom in all of their classes. Faculty over age 65 were also somewhat less likely than others to have used Zoom in all of their classes; 70.59% had done so.

Faculty Requests for Info Technology Assistance, Pre-Pandemic

We asked: prior to the pandemic about how many times in the following periods have you sought the assistance of or otherwise interacted with a member of the Information Technology Staff at your law school, either in person or by phone, Skype, Zoom, email or other means?

The mean was 5.13 with a range of 0 to 50.

Faculty Requests for Info Technology Assistance, Post-Pandemic

Then we asked: How many times did you seek the assistance of or otherwise interacted with a member of the Information Technology Staff at your law school, either in person or by phone, Skype, Zoom, email or other means from March 2020 to March 2021 (During Pandemic)?

The number of consultations in increased significantly to a mean of 12.07, a leap of more than 135%. Older faculty were particularly apt to increase consultations with an increase to a mean of 21.7 from 7.83, an increase of more than 177%. At private college law schools consultations increased to a mean of 15.84 from 5.77 the prior year, an increase of 187%.

Hours Required to Prepare Initial Online Class

We asked: If you taught a course online during the pandemic, how much time in total hours did it take you to prepare this course the first time that you taught it?

The mean was 97.23 with a range of 1 to 1000 and a median of 40. In general, it took longer for faculty from more highly ranked schools and for faculty other than full professors and adjuncts. Also, the older the faculty member, the more time it took them to prepare the initial class online. For those age 44 or under it took a mean of 68 hours, rising to 85 hours for those aged 45-54 and to 99.72 for those aged 55-65 and finally to 116.79 for those over age 65. It also took far longer for males than females; 108.74 to 68.74. Also, the larger a school's enrollment, the more time it took for an instructor to develop a course.

Hours Required to Prepare Subsequent Online Class

We asked: If you taught or soon will teach this predominantly or completely online course a second time, how much time in hours did it or will it take for you to prepare it?

The mean was 45.31 hours with a range of 0 to 500 hours and a median of 20. The average amount of time taken to prepare an online class fell by more than 50%. Online legal education has a significant learning curve and one would expect that, as instructors get more experience, that the time investment required will fall further. Consequently, any new or additional online instruction measures should cost significantly less in the future than they have in the past, in terms of staff time, and needed support services, opening up new versatility and possibilities.

Ease of Integrating Course Content into Course Management System

We asked: In your online classes how easy is it to integrate course content into your course management system or other online system used to serve your students?

We gave five possible answers to this multiple choice question, which were: Very easy, Easy, Neither easy nor difficult, Difficult, Very difficult.

A plurality of 36.70% found integrating course content into their course management system easy while an additional 15.6% found it very easy. However, 16,51% found it difficult, 2,75% very difficult and 17.43%, neither easy nor difficult. It seems that close to 40% of faculty were having troubles to some degree in this area. Faculty at highly ranked law schools, and adjunct and other faculty under the rank of full professor were also more likely than most to encounter difficulties.

Older faculty were also particularly prone to problems, as 27% of faculty aged 55-65 found it difficult and another 5.41%, very difficult. Experience in teaching mattered; the greater the number of courses taught, the lower the percentage of faculty with issues. Only 8.33% of faculty who taught more than two courses in the past semester had significant difficulties.

Integration of Law Library Materials into Online Classes

We asked: Have you integrated information available at your academic library into the course management system or other online system for your students?

We gave three possible answers to this multiple choice question, which were:
Yes No No, but I would like to

A plurality of 46.79% said that they had not integrate information into the course management or other online system for their classes and only 33.94% had done so. A further 9.17% said that they would like to do so. Adjunct and clinical faculty were especially interested in learning how to do it as 18.42% were not currently doing so but wanted to. Women were more likely than men to integrate library info into their course management or other online system and also more likely to want to if they currently were not doing so.

Faculty at public colleges were more likely than those at private ones to have done such integration – 43,48% vs. 26.98%.

Perceived Quality of Online Legal Education

We asked: What is the educational quality of the online courses that you have taught relative to in-person courses?

We gave five possible answers to this multiple choice question, which were:
Much better Better About the same Worse Much worse.

Faculty generally believe that online education has not been as effective as in-person education. 38.53% said that the education quality was about the same in comparison to 35.78% that said it was worse and 2.75% much worse. In contrast, only 8.26% said it was better and 2.75%, much better.

Faculty at the more highly rated schools were more likely than others at lower ranked schools to say that online instruction was worse than in-person instruction. 40% of those in top 20 law schools said it was worse and 5% much worse than in-person instruction. For schools ranked below 80, only 27.59% considered it worse and 3.4% much worse than in-person instruction.

Level of Interest in Post Pandemic Online Teaching

We asked: Post pandemic what percentage of courses that you teach would you like to teach predominantly online?

The mean was 28.47% with a range of 0 to 100% At the more highly ranked schools this percentage floated around 20% while at the lower ranked schools, it averaged about 35.5% One interesting data point: for those in the faculty "other" category, primarily administrators who also may teach, the mean was 62.5% while for full professors it was only 20% -- and for all others somewhere in between. This may be an indicator of an administrator vs. full professor conflict over this issue at some law schools.

Gender was also an issue as women wanted to teach 40.42% of their classes online while men wanted to teach only 23.93% of their classes online.

Another interesting finding is that the median percentage of classes that faculty want to teach online is for almost all categories and breakouts – is zero! Yet the mean is 28.47% which indicates that most faculty want nothing to do with online teaching but that a substantial minority want to teach many if not all of their classes online, another potentially problematic dichotomy.

Law School Plans for Online Teaching

We asked: How would you characterize your law school's plans for post pandemic online teaching?

We gave five possible answers to this multiple choice question, which were: Eliminate online as much as possible Generally go back to our pre-pandemic practices Not as much as now but more than before Much more than before Not really sure

About 10.1% said eliminate as much as possible while 28.44% suggested going back to pre-pandemic practices and 27.52% said more than pre-COVID but not as much as during the pandemic. Females were much more certain than males that their schools' plans included more online teaching than prior to the pandemic with nearly 47% expecting an increase vs. only a bit less than 25% of men expecting an increase over pre-pandemic usage.

We asked: To what extent do you feel that your law school will use online education post pandemic?

We gave four possible answers to this multiple choice question, which were: Less than before the pandemic About as much as before the pandemic More than before the pandemic Much more than before the pandemic

A majority of 55.05% felt that their law school will use online education more than before the pandemic while 3.67% felt it would be much more than before the pandemic.

Classes Most & Least Amenable to Online Teaching

We asked: Which law school courses are most and least amenable to online teaching?

In general small classes and seminars were viewed as most amenable while clinical classes and first year student courses were often seen as more difficult to stage online. Many emphasized the preparedness of instructors rather than the course content or audience as the determining factor. One interesting caveat;

some thought a class that used a great deal of interactive technology, i.e. whiteboards, was more difficult to hold online, others thought this made it less so.

New Courses and Programs Made Possible with Distance Learning in Legal Education

We asked: What new programs or courses do you think the law school has or may now be able to develop now that faculty is more familiar with distance education?

Most answers emphasized specialty areas such as executive education, certificate programs and seminars, and international law student education. Another was remote tech as applied to legal endeavors in general, as online counsel, consultations and witness appearances more frequently take online forms. Another area: evening programs for students working or otherwise engaged during the day. Programs that rely on outside speakers such as issue-specific seminars, also should be easier to stage since speakers will not have to appear on-site.

Evaluation of Need for and Desirability of Online Education in the Future

We asked: What percentage of law school classes do you feel should remain predominantly online post pandemic? The wording of this question differed slightly from the last one and emphasized the survey responders personal preference rather than the actual perceived plans of the law school.

The mean was 17.48% with a range of 0 to 100. Assistant and associate faculty were more enthusiastic than others, perhaps because they are more anxious than the tenured or never to be tenured for the time savings that online teaching can sometimes provide to those who master it. They wanted to see nearly 30% of classes online vs only 14.36% for professors and 18.75% for adjunct faculty. Emeritus faculty also had a higher than average interest in online classes and hoped that 32% of their classes would be online. Once again women were much more interested in men, hoping that a mean of 26.58% of their classes would be online; the same figure for men was 13.11%.

Pandemic-Era Practices that Should be Held Over

What practices that developed during the pandemic do you feel should be held over and extended post pandemic?

Many commented that they liked an in-person/online option for many classes; many also appreciated Zoom office hours and make up classes and the use of online resources for breakout sessions from a main, in-person class.

Table 1.1 Have you used Zoom in any of your courses over the past year?

	Yes in all of them	Yes in some of them	No	No answer
Entire sample	80.73%	4.59%	5.50%	9.17%

Table 1.2 Have you used Zoom in any of your courses over the past year? Broken out by law school ranking

Law school ranking	Yes in all of them	Yes in some of them	No	No answer
Top 20	85.00%	0.00%	5.00%	10.00%
21-45	86.67%	3.33%	0.00%	10.00%
46-80	90.00%	6.67%	3.33%	0.00%
More than 80	62.07%	6.90%	13.79%	17.24%

Table 1.3 Have you used Zoom in any of your courses over the past year? Broken out by title of respondent

Title of respondent	Yes in all of them	Yes in some of them	No	No answer
Professor	75.51%	6.12%	6.12%	12.24%
Assistant/Associate Professor/Lecturer or Research Fellow	90.91%	0.00%	9.09%	0.00%
Adjunct/Clinical Faculty	86.84%	5.26%	5.26%	2.63%
Emeritus	40.00%	0.00%	0.00%	60.00%
Other	100.00%	0.00%	0.00%	0.00%

Table 1.4 Have you used Zoom in any of your courses over the past year? Broken out by age of respondent

Age of respondent	Yes in all of them	Yes in some of them	No	No answer
44 or under	80.00%	10.00%	10.00%	0.00%
45-54	89.29%	7.14%	3.57%	0.00%
55-65	83.78%	2.70%	5.41%	8.11%
Over 65	70.59%	2.94%	5.88%	20.59%

Table 1.5 Have you used Zoom in any of your courses over the past year? Broken out by gender of respondent

Gender of respondent	Yes in all of them	Yes in some of them	No	No answer
Male	77.92%	6.49%	5.19%	10.39%
Female	87.50%	0.00%	6.25%	6.25%

Table 1.6 Have you used Zoom in any of your courses over the past year? Broken out by law school student enrollment

Law school student enrollment	Yes in all of them	Yes in some of them	No	No answer
Less than 400	65.22%	4.35%	13.04%	17.39%
400 - 500	79.31%	6.90%	6.90%	6.90%
501 - 750	92.00%	8.00%	0.00%	0.00%
More than 750	84.38%	0.00%	3.13%	12.50%

Table 1.7 Have you used Zoom in any of your courses over the past year? Broken out by public or private status

Public or private status	Yes in all of them	Yes in some of them	No	No answer
Public	82.61%	4.35%	6.52%	6.52%
Private	79.37%	4.76%	4.76%	11.11%

Table 1.8 Have you used Zoom in any of your courses over the past year? Broken out by number of courses taught in the past semester

Number of courses taught in the past semester	Yes in all of them	Yes in some of them	No	No answer
None	55.56%	11.11%	0.00%	33.33%
One	82.00%	4.00%	4.00%	10.00%
Two	81.58%	2.63%	10.53%	5.26%
More than Two	91.67%	8.33%	0.00%	0.00%

Table 2 About how many times in the following periods have you sought the assistance of or otherwise interacted with a member of the Information Technology Staff at your law school, either in person or by phone, Skype, Zoom, email or other means?

Table 2.1.1 How many times did you seek the assistance of or otherwise interacted with a member of the Information Technology Staff at your law school, either in person or by phone, Skype, Zoom, email or other means in the year prior to the pandemic ending March 1, 2020?

	Mean	Median	Minimum	Maximum
Entire sample	5.13	3.00	0.00	50.00

Table 2.1.2 How many times did you seek the assistance of or otherwise interacted with a member of the Information Technology Staff at your law school, either in person or by phone, Skype, Zoom, email or other means from year prior to the pandemic ending March 1, 2020? Broken out by law school ranking

Law school ranking	Mean	Median	Minimum	Maximum
Top 20	3.91	3.00	0.00	10.00
21-45	4.48	2.00	0.00	50.00
46-80	7.54	3.00	0.00	50.00
More than 80	3.65	3.50	0.00	10.00

Table 2.1.3 How many times did you seek the assistance of or otherwise interacted with a member of the Information Technology Staff at your law school, either in person or by phone, Skype, Zoom, email or other means from year prior to the pandemic ending March 1, 2020? Broken out by title of respondent

Title of respondent	Mean	Median	Minimum	Maximum
Professor	6.21	3.00	0.00	50.00
Assistant/Associate Professor/Lecturer or Research Fellow	4.89	5.00	0.00	10.00
Adjunct/Clinical Faculty	2.55	2.00	0.00	20.00
Emeritus	7.00	7.00	4.00	10.00
Other	11.50	4.50	0.00	50.00

Table 2.1.4 How many times did you seek the assistance of or otherwise interacted with a member of the Information Technology Staff at your law school, either in person or by phone, Skype, Zoom, email or other means from year prior to the pandemic ending March 1, 2020? Broken out by age of respondent

Age of respondent	Mean	Median	Minimum	Maximum
44 or under	2.06	1.00	0.00	7.50
45-54	6.02	2.00	0.00	50.00
55-65	3.43	3.00	0.00	10.00
Over 65	7.83	4.00	0.00	50.00

Table 2.1.5 How many times did you seek the assistance of or otherwise interacted with a member of the Information Technology Staff at your law school, either in person or by phone, Skype, Zoom, email or other means from year prior to the pandemic ending March 1, 2020? Broken out by gender of respondent

Gender of respondent	Mean	Median	Minimum	Maximum
Male	4.59	3.00	0.00	50.00
Female	6.31	3.00	0.00	50.00

Table 2.1.6 How many times did you seek the assistance of or otherwise interacted with a member of the Information Technology Staff at your law school, either in person or by phone, Skype, Zoom, email or other means from year prior to the pandemic ending March 1, 2020? Broken out by law school student enrollment

Law school student enrollment	Mean	Median	Minimum	Maximum
Less than 400	6.35	3.00	0.00	50.00
400 - 500	3.57	3.00	0.00	12.00
501 - 750	6.91	1.00	0.00	50.00
More than 750	3.91	4.00	0.00	10.00

Table 2.1.7 How many times did you seek the assistance of or otherwise interacted with a member of the Information Technology Staff at your law school, either in person or by phone, Skype, Zoom, email or other means from year prior to the pandemic ending March 1, 2020? Broken out by public or private status

Public or private status	Mean	Median	Minimum	Maximum
Public	4.32	2.50	0.00	50.00
Private	5.77	3.00	0.00	50.00

Table 2.1.8 How many times did you seek the assistance of or otherwise interacted with a member of the Information Technology Staff at your law school, either in person or by phone, Skype, Zoom, email or other means from year prior to the pandemic ending March 1, 2020? Broken out by number of courses taught in the past semester

Number of courses taught in the past semester	Mean	Median	Minimum	Maximum
None	10.43	4.00	0.00	50.00
One	3.81	2.00	0.00	30.00
Two	3.58	3.00	0.00	12.00
More than Two	11.50	5.00	1.00	50.00

Table 2.2.1 How many times did you seek the assistance of or otherwise interacted with a member of the Information Technology Staff at your law school, either in person or by phone, Skype, Zoom, email or other means from March 2020 to March 2021 (During Pandemic)?

	Mean	Median	Minimum	Maximum
Entire sample	12.07	5.50	0.00	200.00

Table 2.2.2 How many times did you seek the assistance of or otherwise interacted with a member of the Information Technology Staff at your law school, either in person or by phone, Skype, Zoom, email or other means from March 2020 to March 2021 (During Pandemic)? Broken out by law school ranking

Law school ranking	Mean	Median	Minimum	Maximum
Top 20	10.68	10.00	2.00	30.00
21-45	7.81	5.00	0.00	40.00
46-80	22.00	5.00	0.00	200.00
More than 80	5.95	5.00	0.00	20.00

Table 2.2.3 How many times did you seek the assistance of or otherwise interacted with a member of the Information Technology Staff at your law school, either in person or by phone, Skype, Zoom, email or other means from March 2020 to March 2021 (During Pandemic)? Broken out by title of respondent

Title of respondent	Mean	Median	Minimum	Maximum
Professor	14.71	6.00	0.00	200.00
Assistant/Associate Professor/Lecturer or Research Fellow	9.28	7.50	0.00	30.00
Adjunct/Clinical Faculty	7.83	4.00	0.00	50.00
Emeritus	13.00	13.00	6.00	20.00
Other	21.67	11.50	3.00	80.00

Table 2.2.4 How many times did you seek the assistance of or otherwise interacted with a member of the Information Technology Staff at your law school, either in person or by phone, Skype, Zoom, email or other means from March 2020 to March 2021 (During Pandemic)? Broken out by age of respondent

Age of respondent	Mean	Median	Minimum	Maximum
44 or under	4.78	3.00	0.00	15.00
45-54	12.13	5.00	0.00	80.00
55-65	7.33	5.00	0.00	40.00
Over 65	21.67	10.00	0.00	200.00

Table 2.2.5 How many times did you seek the assistance of or otherwise interacted with a member of the Information Technology Staff at your law school, either in person or by phone, Skype, Zoom, email or other means from March 2020 to March 2021 (During Pandemic)? Broken out by gender of respondent

Gender of respondent	Mean	Median	Minimum	Maximum
Male	11.42	6.00	0.00	200.00
Female	13.46	5.00	0.00	80.00

Table 2.2.6 How many times did you seek the assistance of or otherwise interacted with a member of the Information Technology Staff at your law school, either in person or by phone, Skype, Zoom, email or other means from March 2020 to March 2021 (During Pandemic)? Broken out by law school student enrollment

Law school student enrollment	Mean	Median	Minimum	Maximum
Less than 400	15.24	10.00	0.00	80.00
400 - 500	6.81	5.00	0.00	24.00
501 - 750	10.32	4.50	0.00	60.00
More than 750	16.39	6.75	1.00	200.00

Table 2.2.7 How many times did you seek the assistance of or otherwise interacted with a member of the Information Technology Staff at your law school, either in person or by phone, Skype, Zoom, email or other means from March 2020 to March 2021 (During Pandemic)? Broken out by public or private status

Public or private status	Mean	Median	Minimum	Maximum
Public	7.25	4.50	0.00	40.00
Private	15.84	9.50	0.00	200.00

Table 2.2.8 How many times did you seek the assistance of or otherwise interacted with a member of the Information Technology Staff at your law school, either in person or by phone, Skype, Zoom, email or other means from March 2020 to March 2021 (During Pandemic)? Broken out by number of courses taught in the past semester

Number of courses taught in the past semester	Mean	Median	Minimum	Maximum
None	17.14	6.00	0.00	80.00
One	9.17	5.00	0.00	60.00
Two	13.85	6.00	0.00	200.00
More than Two	13.22	10.00	2.00	50.00

Table 3.1 If you taught a course online during the pandemic, how much time in total hours did it take you to prepare this course the first time that you taught it?

	Mean	Median	Minimum	Maximum
Entire sample	97.23	40.00	1.00	1000.00

Table 3.2 If you taught a course online during the pandemic, how much time in total hours did it take you to prepare this course the first time that you taught it? Broken out by law school ranking

Law school ranking	Mean	Median	Minimum	Maximum
Top 20	140.60	32.50	6.00	1000.00
21-45	100.81	40.00	1.00	1000.00
46-80	79.70	45.00	3.00	300.00
More than 80	87.73	75.00	3.00	240.00

Table 3.3 If you taught a course online during the pandemic, how much time in total hours did it take you to prepare this course the first time that you taught it? Broken out by title of respondent

Title of respondent	Mean	Median	Minimum	Maximum
Professor	126.39	75.00	3.00	1000.00
Assistant/Associate Professor/Lecturer or Research Fellow	274.00	150.00	4.00	1000.00
Adjunct/Clinical Faculty	45.30	30.00	1.00	150.00
Emeritus	3.00	3.00	3.00	3.00
Other	22.25	8.00	3.00	70.00

Table 3.4 If you taught a course online during the pandemic, how much time in total hours did it take you to prepare this course the first time that you taught it? Broken out by age of respondent

Age of respondent	Mean	Median	Minimum	Maximum
44 or under	68.00	9.00	2.00	300.00
45-54	85.03	80.00	1.00	250.00
55-65	99.72	40.00	3.00	1000.00
Over 65	116.79	40.00	3.00	1000.00

Table 3.5 If you taught a course online during the pandemic, how much time in total hours did it take you to prepare this course the first time that you taught it? Broken out by gender of respondent

Gender of respondent	Mean	Median	Minimum	Maximum
Male	108.74	40.00	1.00	1000.00
Female	68.74	40.00	2.00	300.00

Table 3.6 If you taught a course online during the pandemic, how much time in total hours did it take you to prepare this course the first time that you taught it? Broken out by law school student enrollment

Law school student enrollment	Mean	Median	Minimum	Maximum
Less than 400	63.82	32.50	3.00	300.00
400 - 500	74.33	40.00	2.00	250.00
501 - 750	105.00	27.50	1.00	1000.00
More than 750	146.62	75.00	6.00	1000.00

Table 3.7 If you taught a course online during the pandemic, how much time in total hours did it take you to prepare this course the first time that you taught it? Broken out by public or private status

Public or private status	Mean	Median	Minimum	Maximum
Public	97.34	40.00	1.00	1000.00
Private	97.11	40.00	3.00	1000.00

Table 3.8 If you taught a course online during the pandemic, how much time in total hours did it take you to prepare this course the first time that you taught it? Broken out by number of courses taught in the past semester

Number of courses taught in the past semester	Mean	Median	Minimum	Maximum
None	16.50	16.50	3.00	30.00
One	49.21	40.00	2.00	200.00
Two	136.65	100.00	1.00	1000.00
More than Two	171.55	30.00	5.00	1000.00

Table 4.1 If you taught or soon will teach this predominantly or completely online course a second time, how much time in hours did it or will it take for you to prepare it?

	Mean	Median	Minimum	Maximum
Entire sample	45.31	20.00	0.00	500.00

Table 4.2 If you taught or soon will teach this predominantly or completely online course a second time, how much time in hours did it or will it take for you to prepare it? Broken out by law school ranking

Law school ranking	Mean	Median	Minimum	Maximum
Top 20	70.15	21.25	0.00	500.00
21-45	51.81	20.00	0.00	500.00
46-80	30.57	13.50	2.00	150.00
More than 80	40.67	25.00	1.50	100.00

Table 4.3 If you taught or soon will teach this predominantly or completely online course a second time, how much time in hours did it or will it take for you to prepare it? Broken out by title of respondent

Title of respondent	Mean	Median	Minimum	Maximum
Professor	56.48	20.00	0.00	500.00
Assistant/Associate Professor/Lecturer or Research Fellow	117.33	45.00	4.00	500.00
Adjunct/Clinical Faculty	23.53	17.50	0.00	100.00
Emeritus	1.50	1.50	1.50	1.50
Other	25.38	5.00	1.50	90.00

Table 4.4 If you taught or soon will teach this predominantly or completely online course a second time, how much time in hours did it or will it take for you to prepare it? Broken out by age of respondent

Age of respondent	Mean	Median	Minimum	Maximum
44 or under	25.25	4.00	2.00	100.00
45-54	34.52	23.75	0.00	150.00
55-65	53.54	25.00	1.50	500.00
Over 65	52.89	20.00	0.00	500.00

Table 4.5 If you taught or soon will teach this predominantly or completely online course a second time, how much time in hours did it or will it take for you to prepare it? Broken out by gender of respondent

Gender of respondent	Mean	Median	Minimum	Maximum
Male	51.69	20.00	0.00	500.00
Female	29.55	16.00	2.00	100.00

Table 4.6 If you taught or soon will teach this predominantly or completely online course a second time, how much time in hours did it or will it take for you to prepare it? Broken out by law school student enrollment

Law school student enrollment	Mean	Median	Minimum	Maximum
Less than 400	23.88	12.00	1.00	80.00
400 - 500	40.12	20.00	0.00	150.00
501 - 750	53.25	15.00	1.00	500.00
More than 750	62.85	40.00	0.00	500.00

Table 4.7 If you taught or soon will teach this predominantly or completely online course a second time, how much time in hours did it or will it take for you to prepare it? Broken out by public or private status

Public or private status	Mean	Median	Minimum	Maximum
Public	51.40	20.00	0.00	500.00
Private	38.84	20.00	0.00	500.00

Table 4.8 If you taught or soon will teach this predominantly or completely online course a second time, how much time in hours did it or will it take for you to prepare it? Broken out by number of courses taught in the past semester

Number of courses taught in the past semester	Mean	Median	Minimum	Maximum
None	20.75	20.75	1.50	40.00
One	25.91	20.00	0.00	100.00
Two	62.54	30.00	1.00	500.00
More than Two	70.75	10.50	0.00	500.00

Table 5.1 In your online classes how easy is it to integrate course content into your course management system or other online system used to serve your students?

	Very easy	Easy	Neither easy nor difficult	Difficult	Very difficult	No answer
Entire sample	15.60%	36.70%	17.43%	16.51%	2.75%	11.01%

Table 5.2 In your online classes how easy is it to integrate course content into your course management system or other online system used to serve your students? Broken out by law school ranking

Law school ranking	Very easy	Easy	Neither easy nor difficult	Difficult	Very difficult	No answer
Top 20	15.00%	40.00%	10.00%	25.00%	0.00%	10.00%
21-45	10.00%	43.33%	20.00%	16.67%	0.00%	10.00%
46-80	20.00%	40.00%	20.00%	13.33%	3.33%	3.33%
More than 80	17.24%	24.14%	17.24%	13.79%	6.90%	20.69%

Table 5.3 In your online classes how easy is it to integrate course content into your course management system or other online system used to serve your students? Broken out by title of respondent

Title of respondent	Very easy	Easy	Neither easy nor difficult	Difficult	Very difficult	No answer
Professor	18.37%	46.94%	12.24%	8.16%	2.04%	12.24%
Assistant/Associate Professor/Lecturer or Research Fellow	18.18%	45.45%	9.09%	27.27%	0.00%	0.00%
Adjunct/Clinical Faculty	13.16%	26.32%	23.68%	26.32%	5.26%	5.26%
Emeritus	20.00%	0.00%	0.00%	20.00%	0.00%	60.00%
Other	0.00%	33.33%	50.00%	0.00%	0.00%	16.67%

Table 5.4 In your online classes how easy is it to integrate course content into your course management system or other online system used to serve your students? Broken out by age of respondent

Age of respondent	Very easy	Easy	Neither easy nor difficult	Difficult	Very difficult	No answer
44 or under	30.00%	50.00%	10.00%	10.00%	0.00%	0.00%
45-54	14.29%	50.00%	25.00%	0.00%	3.57%	7.14%
55-65	10.81%	29.73%	18.92%	27.03%	5.41%	8.11%
Over 65	17.65%	29.41%	11.76%	20.59%	0.00%	20.59%

Table 5.5 In your online classes how easy is it to integrate course content into your course management system or other online system used to serve your students? Broken out by gender of respondent

Gender of respondent	Very easy	Easy	Neither easy nor difficult	Difficult	Very difficult	No answer
Male	14.29%	38.96%	15.58%	16.88%	3.90%	10.39%
Female	18.75%	31.25%	21.88%	15.63%	0.00%	12.50%

Table 5.6 In your online classes how easy is it to integrate course content into your course management system or other online system used to serve your students? Broken out by law school student enrollment

Law school student enrollment	Very easy	Easy	Neither easy nor difficult	Difficult	Very difficult	No answer
Less than 400	13.04%	26.09%	17.39%	17.39%	4.35%	21.74%
400 - 500	6.90%	41.38%	24.14%	17.24%	3.45%	6.90%
501 - 750	16.00%	36.00%	24.00%	20.00%	4.00%	0.00%
More than 750	25.00%	40.63%	6.25%	12.50%	0.00%	15.63%

Table 5.7 In your online classes how easy is it to integrate course content into your course management system or other online system used to serve your students? Broken out by public or private status

Public or private status	Very easy	Easy	Neither easy nor difficult	Difficult	Very difficult	No answer
Public	6.52%	47.83%	21.74%	15.22%	2.17%	6.52%
Private	22.22%	28.57%	14.29%	17.46%	3.17%	14.29%

Table 5.8 In your online classes how easy is it to integrate course content into your course management system or other online system used to serve your students? Broken out by number of courses taught in the past semester

Number of courses taught in the past semester	Very easy	Easy	Neither easy nor difficult	Difficult	Very difficult	No answer
None	0.00%	0.00%	11.11%	22.22%	11.11%	55.56%
One	14.00%	30.00%	22.00%	22.00%	2.00%	10.00%
Two	18.42%	47.37%	15.79%	10.53%	2.63%	5.26%
More than Two	25.00%	58.33%	8.33%	8.33%	0.00%	0.00%

Table 6.1 Have you integrated information available at your academic library into the course management system or other online system for your students?

	Yes	No	No but I would like to	No answer
Entire sample	33.94%	46.79%	9.17%	10.09%

Table 6.2 Have you integrated information available at your academic library into the course management system or other online system for your students? Broken out by law school ranking

Law school ranking	Yes	No	No but I would like to	No answer
Top 20	25.00%	55.00%	10.00%	10.00%
21-45	36.67%	46.67%	6.67%	10.00%
46-80	46.67%	40.00%	10.00%	3.33%
More than 80	24.14%	48.28%	10.34%	17.24%

Table 6.3 Have you integrated information available at your academic library into the course management system or other online system for your students? Broken out by title of respondent

Title of respondent	Yes	No	No but I would like to	No answer
Professor	38.78%	44.90%	4.08%	12.24%
Assistant/Associate Professor/Lecturer or Research Fellow	54.55%	36.36%	9.09%	0.00%
Adjunct/Clinical Faculty	28.95%	47.37%	18.42%	5.26%
Emeritus	0.00%	40.00%	0.00%	60.00%
Other	16.67%	83.33%	0.00%	0.00%

Table 6.4 Have you integrated information available at your academic library into the course management system or other online system for your students? Broken out by age of respondent

Age of respondent	Yes	No	No but I would like to	No answer
44 or under	20.00%	70.00%	10.00%	0.00%
45-54	39.29%	50.00%	7.14%	3.57%
55-65	51.35%	32.43%	8.11%	8.11%
Over 65	14.71%	52.94%	11.76%	20.59%

Table 6.5 Have you integrated information available at your academic library into the course management system or other online system for your students? Broken out by gender of respondent

Gender of respondent	Yes	No	No but I would like to	No answer
Male	31.17%	49.35%	7.79%	11.69%
Female	40.63%	40.63%	12.50%	6.25%

Table 6.6 Have you integrated information available at your academic library into the course management system or other online system for your students? Broken out by law school student enrollment

Law school student enrollment	Yes	No	No but I would like to	No answer
Less than 400	30.43%	43.48%	8.70%	17.39%
400 - 500	37.93%	48.28%	3.45%	10.34%
501 - 750	36.00%	48.00%	16.00%	0.00%
More than 750	31.25%	46.88%	9.38%	12.50%

Table 6.7 Have you integrated information available at your academic library into the course management system or other online system for your students? Broken out by public or private status

Public or private status	Yes	No	No but I would like to	No answer
Public	43.48%	39.13%	8.70%	8.70%
Private	26.98%	52.38%	9.52%	11.11%

Table 6.8 Have you integrated information available at your academic library into the course management system or other online system for your students? Broken out by number of courses taught in the past semester

Number of courses taught in the past semester	Yes	No	No but I would like to	No answer
None	0.00%	55.56%	11.11%	33.33%
One	32.00%	50.00%	6.00%	12.00%
Two	44.74%	34.21%	15.79%	5.26%
More than Two	33.33%	66.67%	0.00%	0.00%

Table 7.1 What is the educational quality of the online courses that you have taught relative to in-person courses?

	Much better	Better	About the same	Worse	Much worse	No answer
Entire sample	2.75%	8.26%	38.53%	35.78%	2.75%	11.93%

Table 7.2 What is the educational quality of the online courses that you have taught relative to in-person courses? Broken out by law school ranking

Law school ranking	Much better	Better	About the same	Worse	Much worse	No answer
Top 20	0.00%	10.00%	35.00%	40.00%	5.00%	10.00%
21-45	3.33%	3.33%	36.67%	43.33%	3.33%	10.00%
46-80	6.67%	13.33%	40.00%	33.33%	0.00%	6.67%
More than 80	0.00%	6.90%	41.38%	27.59%	3.45%	20.69%

Table 7.3 What is the educational quality of the online courses that you have taught relative to in-person courses? Broken out by title of respondent

Title of respondent	Much better	Better	About the same	Worse	Much worse	No answer
Professor	6.12%	6.12%	32.65%	36.73%	4.08%	14.29%
Assistant/Associate Professor/Lecturer or Research Fellow	0.00%	27.27%	36.36%	27.27%	9.09%	0.00%
Adjunct/Clinical Faculty	0.00%	5.26%	52.63%	36.84%	0.00%	5.26%
Emeritus	0.00%	0.00%	20.00%	20.00%	0.00%	60.00%
Other	0.00%	16.67%	16.67%	50.00%	0.00%	16.67%

Table 7.4 What is the educational quality of the online courses that you have taught relative to in-person courses? Broken out by age of respondent

Age of respondent	Much better	Better	About the same	Worse	Much worse	No answer
44 or under	0.00%	30.00%	30.00%	40.00%	0.00%	0.00%
45-54	0.00%	7.14%	46.43%	35.71%	3.57%	7.14%
55-65	2.70%	10.81%	35.14%	40.54%	2.70%	8.11%
Over 65	5.88%	0.00%	38.24%	29.41%	2.94%	23.53%

Table 7.5 What is the educational quality of the online courses that you have taught relative to in-person courses? Broken out by gender of respondent

Gender of respondent	Much better	Better	About the same	Worse	Much worse	No answer
Male	3.90%	2.60%	36.36%	42.86%	2.60%	11.69%
Female	0.00%	21.88%	43.75%	18.75%	3.13%	12.50%

Table 7.6 What is the educational quality of the online courses that you have taught relative to in-person courses? Broken out by law school student enrollment

Law school student enrollment	Much better	Better	About the same	Worse	Much worse	No answer
Less than 400	0.00%	0.00%	43.48%	30.43%	4.35%	21.74%
400 - 500	0.00%	13.79%	27.59%	51.72%	0.00%	6.90%
501 - 750	4.00%	0.00%	44.00%	40.00%	8.00%	4.00%
More than 750	6.25%	15.63%	40.63%	21.88%	0.00%	15.63%

Table 7.7 What is the educational quality of the online courses that you have taught relative to in-person courses? Broken out by public or private status

Public or private status	Much better	Better	About the same	Worse	Much worse	No answer
Public	2.17%	10.87%	41.30%	39.13%	0.00%	6.52%
Private	3.17%	6.35%	36.51%	33.33%	4.76%	15.87%

Table 7.8 What is the educational quality of the online courses that you have taught relative to in-person courses? Broken out by number of courses taught in the past semester

Number of courses taught in the past semester	Much better	Better	About the same	Worse	Much worse	No answer
None	0.00%	0.00%	0.00%	44.44%	0.00%	55.56%
One	0.00%	8.00%	38.00%	40.00%	2.00%	12.00%
Two	2.63%	10.53%	47.37%	28.95%	5.26%	5.26%
More than Two	16.67%	8.33%	41.67%	33.33%	0.00%	0.00%

Table 8.1 Post pandemic what percentage of courses that you teach would you like to teach predominantly online?

	Mean	Median	Minimum	Maximum
Entire sample	28.47	0.00	0.00	100.00

Table 8.2 Post pandemic what percentage of courses that you teach would you like to teach predominantly online? Broken out by law school ranking

Law school ranking	Mean	Median	Minimum	Maximum
Top 20	20.50	0.00	0.00	100.00
21-45	18.65	0.00	0.00	100.00
46-80	35.07	20.00	0.00	100.00
More than 80	36.11	25.00	0.00	100.00

Table 8.3 Post pandemic what percentage of courses that you teach would you like to teach predominantly online? Broken out by title of respondent

Title of respondent	Mean	Median	Minimum	Maximum
Professor	20.53	0.00	0.00	100.00
Assistant/Associate Professor/Lecturer or Research Fellow	41.57	50.00	0.00	100.00
Adjunct/Clinical Faculty	34.58	2.50	0.00	100.00
Emeritus	0.00	0.00	0.00	0.00
Other	62.50	62.50	50.00	75.00

Table 8.4 Post pandemic what percentage of courses that you teach would you like to teach predominantly online? Broken out by age of respondent

Age of respondent	Mean	Median	Minimum	Maximum
44 or under	31.25	25.00	0.00	100.00
45-54	26.20	5.00	0.00	100.00
55-65	29.20	0.00	0.00	100.00
Over 65	28.78	0.00	0.00	100.00

Table 8.5 Post pandemic what percentage of courses that you teach would you like to teach predominantly online? Broken out by gender of respondent

Gender of respondent	Mean	Median	Minimum	Maximum
Male	23.93	0.00	0.00	100.00
Female	40.42	33.00	0.00	100.00

Table 8.6 Post pandemic what percentage of courses that you teach would you like to teach predominantly online? Broken out by law school student enrollment

Law school student enrollment	Mean	Median	Minimum	Maximum
Less than 400	40.91	0.00	0.00	100.00
400 - 500	23.00	0.00	0.00	100.00
501 - 750	18.48	0.00	0.00	100.00
More than 750	43.32	32.50	0.00	100.00

Table 8.7 Post pandemic what percentage of courses that you teach would you like to teach predominantly online? Broken out by public or private status

Public or private status	Mean	Median	Minimum	Maximum
Public	28.45	0.00	0.00	100.00
Private	28.49	0.00	0.00	100.00

Table 8.8 Post pandemic what percentage of courses that you teach would you like to teach predominantly online? Broken out by number of courses taught in the past semester

Number of courses taught in the past semester	Mean	Median	Minimum	Maximum
None	0.00	0.00	0.00	0.00
One	35.21	0.00	0.00	100.00
Two	21.75	0.00	0.00	100.00
More than Two	34.36	20.00	0.00	100.00

Table 9.1 How would you characterize your law school's plans for post pandemic online teaching?

	Eliminate online as much as possible	Generally go back to our pre-pandemic practices	Not as much as now but more than before	Much more than before	Not really sure	No answer
Entire sample	10.09%	28.44%	27.52%	3.67%	20.18%	10.09%

Table 9.2 How would you characterize your law school's plans for post pandemic online teaching? Broken out by law school ranking

Law school ranking	Eliminate online as much as possible	Generally go back to our pre-pandemic practices	Not as much as now but more than before	Much more than before	Not really sure	No answer
Top 20	25.00%	40.00%	10.00%	0.00%	10.00%	15.00%
21-45	6.67%	23.33%	26.67%	0.00%	33.33%	10.00%
46-80	0.00%	23.33%	40.00%	10.00%	23.33%	3.33%
More than 80	13.79%	31.03%	27.59%	3.45%	10.34%	13.79%

Table 9.3 How would you characterize your law school's plans for post pandemic online teaching? Broken out by title of respondent

Title of respondent	Eliminate online as much as possible	Generally go back to our pre-pandemic practices	Not as much as now but more than before	Much more than before	Not really sure	No answer
Professor	12.24%	26.53%	32.65 %	2.04%	14.29 %	12.24 %
Assistant/Associate Professor/Lecturer or Research Fellow	0.00%	54.55%	27.27 %	0.00%	18.18 %	0.00%
Adjunct/Clinical Faculty	7.89%	26.32%	21.05 %	5.26%	34.21 %	5.26%
Emeritus	20.00%	20.00%	0.00%	20.00 %	0.00%	40.00 %
Other	16.67%	16.67%	50.00 %	0.00%	0.00%	16.67 %

Table 9.4 How would you characterize your law school's plans for post pandemic online teaching? Broken out by age of respondent

Age of respondent	Eliminate online as much as possible	Generally go back to our pre-pandemic practices	Not as much as now but more than before	Much more than before	Not really sure	No answer
44 or under	0.00%	60.00%	10.00%	10.00%	20.00%	0.00%
45-54	7.14%	14.29%	50.00%	0.00%	25.00%	3.57%
55-65	13.51%	32.43%	18.92%	2.70%	21.62%	10.81%
Over 65	11.76%	26.47%	23.53%	5.88%	14.71%	17.65%

Table 9.5 How would you characterize your law school's plans for post pandemic online teaching? Broken out by gender of respondent

Gender of respondent	Eliminate online as much as possible	Generally go back to our pre-pandemic practices	Not as much as now but more than before	Much more than before	Not really sure	No answer
Male	11.69%	31.17%	22.08%	2.60%	22.08%	10.39%
Female	6.25%	21.88%	40.63%	6.25%	15.63%	9.38%

Table 9.6 How would you characterize your law school's plans for post pandemic online teaching? Broken out by law school student enrollment

Law school student enrollment	Eliminate online as much as possible	Generally go back to our pre-pandemic practices	Not as much as now but more than before	Much more than before	Not really sure	No answer
Less than 400	8.70%	26.09%	26.09%	4.35%	17.39%	17.39%
400 - 500	10.34%	31.03%	27.59%	0.00%	24.14%	6.90%
501 - 750	8.00%	28.00%	36.00%	0.00%	24.00%	4.00%
More than 750	12.50%	28.13%	21.88%	9.38%	15.63%	12.50%

Table 9.7 How would you characterize your law school's plans for post pandemic online teaching? Broken out by public or private status

Public or private status	Eliminate online as much as possible	Generally go back to our pre-pandemic practices	Not as much as now but more than before	Much more than before	Not really sure	No answer
Public	6.52%	21.74%	36.96%	2.17%	26.09%	6.52%
Private	12.70%	33.33%	20.63%	4.76%	15.87%	12.70%

Table 9.8 How would you characterize your law school's plans for post pandemic online teaching? Broken out by number of courses taught in the past semester

Number of courses taught in the past semester	Eliminate online as much as possible	Generally go back to our pre-pandemic practices	Not as much as now but more than before	Much more than before	Not really sure	No answer
None	11.11%	22.22%	0.00%	11.11%	11.11%	44.44%
One	6.00%	26.00%	24.00%	2.00%	32.00%	10.00%
Two	15.79%	28.95%	39.47%	5.26%	5.26%	5.26%
More than Two	8.33%	41.67%	25.00%	0.00%	25.00%	0.00%

Not really sure:

1. No info
2. Management hasn't told faculty anything about this
3. We are in the course of those discussions now
4. No idea at this point.
5. not really sure
6. The question is unintelligible
7. No need to comment
8. unsure
9. The administration is giving us no information
10. I haven't heard this announced (I am only an adjunct!!)

11. Don't know. The school hasn't made a decision, as far as I'm aware.
12. Not sure
13. They are bounding from crisis to crisis with no long range plan.
14. But very effective leadership - will certainly makes effort to incorporate the better aspects of zoom etc.
15. No idea what they are planning
16. I don't know the plans.
17. don't know
18. Don't know
19. no opinion
20. we don't know yet
21. don't know, I'm an adjunct

Table 10.1 To what extent do you feel that your law school will use online education post pandemic?

	Less than before the pandemic	About as much as before the pandemic	More than before the pandemic	Much more than before the pandemic	No answer
Entire sample	8.26%	23.85%	55.05%	3.67%	9.17%

Table 10.2 To what extent do you feel that your law school will use online education post pandemic? Broken out by law school ranking

Law school ranking	Less than before the pandemic	About as much as before the pandemic	More than before the pandemic	Much more than before the pandemic	No answer
Top 20	5.00%	25.00%	50.00%	5.00%	15.00%
21-45	16.67%	20.00%	53.33%	0.00%	10.00%
46-80	0.00%	20.00%	70.00%	6.67%	3.33%
More than 80	10.34%	31.03%	44.83%	3.45%	10.34%

Table 10.3 To what extent do you feel that your law school will use online education post pandemic? Broken out by title of respondent

0	Less than before the pandemic	About as much as before the pandemic	More than before the pandemic	Much more than before the pandemic	No answer
Professor	6.12%	16.33%	57.14%	8.16%	12.24%
Assistant/Associate Professor/Lecturer or Research Fellow	9.09%	27.27%	63.64%	0.00%	0.00%
Adjunct/Clinical Faculty	10.53%	31.58%	50.00%	0.00%	7.89%
Emeritus	0.00%	40.00%	40.00%	0.00%	20.00%
Other	16.67%	16.67%	66.67%	0.00%	0.00%

Table 10.4 To what extent do you feel that your law school will use online education post pandemic? Broken out by age of respondent

Age of respondent	Less than before the pandemic	About as much as before the pandemic	More than before the pandemic	Much more than before the pandemic	No answer
44 or under	0.00%	40.00%	60.00%	0.00%	0.00%
45-54	10.71%	17.86%	67.86%	3.57%	0.00%
55-65	13.51%	21.62%	51.35%	2.70%	10.81%
Over 65	2.94%	26.47%	47.06%	5.88%	17.65%

Table 10.5 To what extent do you feel that your law school will use online education post pandemic? Broken out by gender of respondent

Gender of respondent	Less than before the pandemic	About as much as before the pandemic	More than before the pandemic	Much more than before the pandemic	No answer
Male	7.79%	25.97%	54.55%	2.60%	9.09%
Female	9.38%	18.75%	56.25%	6.25%	9.38%

Table 10.6 To what extent do you feel that your law school will use online education post pandemic? Broken out by law school student enrollment

Law school student enrollment	Less than before the pandemic	About as much as before the pandemic	More than before the pandemic	Much more than before the pandemic	No answer
Less than 400	8.70%	34.78%	43.48%	0.00%	13.04%
400 - 500	13.79%	27.59%	51.72%	3.45%	3.45%
501 - 750	4.00%	12.00%	68.00%	8.00%	8.00%
More than 750	6.25%	21.88%	56.25%	3.13%	12.50%

Table 10.7 To what extent do you feel that your law school will use online education post pandemic? Broken out by public or private status

Public or private status	Less than before the pandemic	About as much as before the pandemic	More than before the pandemic	Much more than before the pandemic	No answer
Public	13.04%	23.91%	54.35%	2.17%	6.52%
Private	4.76%	23.81%	55.56%	4.76%	11.11%

Table 10.8 To what extent do you feel that your law school will use online education post pandemic? Broken out by number of courses taught in the past semester

Number of courses taught in the past semester	Less than before the pandemic	About as much as before the pandemic	More than before the pandemic	Much more than before the pandemic	No answer
None	11.11%	33.33%	33.33%	0.00%	22.22%
One	10.00%	28.00%	46.00%	4.00%	12.00%
Two	7.89%	18.42%	65.79%	2.63%	5.26%
More than Two	0.00%	16.67%	75.00%	8.33%	0.00%

Which law school courses are most and least amenable to online teaching? Broken out by law school ranking

Top 20

1) Smaller classes (up to 20 students) are most amenable.
2) Most-short subject webinars-most Clinics-least
3) Small seminar-style classes
4) experiential courses
5) clinics
6) Least: 1L courses Most: Small seminars
7) It is bad for all of them. Maybe seminars are the least bad
8) First year courses are terrible online; courses that are more about information transfer work better
9) Most amenable: Big lecture courses Least amenable: Clinics
10) more interactive with white/blackboard, the harder it is to use online.
11) Lecture format easy on line if questions are not vital
12) Large 1L classes have been better
13) 1L courses: Least Seminars: Most

21-45

1) Accounting most Con law least
2) Most: upper-class lecture courses. Least: clinical courses, first-year courses, and discussion-oriented courses.
3) I think this is driven more by the professor and their willing to (effectively) teach online, than it is about the course. I teach a class that has weekly assignments, and I have been able to use polling or online platforms for the class to answer multiple and short answer questions, create breakout rooms for group exercises, and display PowerPoint slides and use a whiteboard.
4) I think that every class is amendable to online teaching if that teaching is done well. What is not "good online teaching" is simply a talking head on zoom.
5) I feel like the clinics benefit most from in-person learning, but also understand the need to keep faculty, students and clients safe.
6) Lecture classes are more amenable to online teaching. Practice based or clinical courses are less amenable.
7) Courses that are taught my adjuncts who lives a long distance away are most amenable to online teaching.
8) 1L classes
9) Clinical Education
10) Least: all first-year courses Most: upper level substantive courses

11) seminars are most amenable. large lecture classes less so.
12) Legal Research courses, Administrative Law courses, Criminal and Tort law courses
13) Online teaching is not a suitable way to teach law school courses. Period.
14) No courses are amendable to online teaching. It should only be used when necessary for non-pedagogical reasons.
15) Surprisingly, experiential courses can be done effectively with zoom and some even more effectively because the students can be anywhere, they learn to go with the flow of the technology and body language is actually much more evident on camera. So when teaching mediation, for example, they have a great chance to learn to "read" faces and react accordingly.
16) Least - Trial Advocacy
17) Most - large lectures
18) 1L Classes, Advocacy Classes
19) Seminar courses are tough to teach via zoom. Hard to develop a good, multiparty, interactive conversation via zoom.
20) Most- lecture courses Least- smaller classes
21) don't know
22) Doctrinal courses probably most amenable, but seminar and writing classes are better in person.

46-80

1) Most = smaller electives. Least = LRW
2) Most: upper-division specialized doctrinal courses Least: experiential courses
3) most, tax; least, first year courses
4) Most-purely didactic courses
5) Most: LLM Least: Clinics
6) 1L are least amenable. Clinical and experiential courses are least amendable.
7) Socratic style courses and seminars are well suited to synchronous on-line delivery. Upper-level survey courses are not amenable to on-line teaching. And few course are truly amenable to asynchronous on-line instruction, at least without massive investments in time and resources to develop.
8) Upper level courses are more amenable. First year courses are least amenable.
9) any lecture classes w questions are amenable, whereas trial advocacy are not.
10) Least - large classes, hands on classes Best - small exam classes
11) not sure
12) disccussoin and seminar classes need to be live lectures even with socratic are oK for zoom
13) All DR courses
14) skills courses least

15) Most - Legal research and writing
16) My courses are very interactive, with a lot of moving in and out of small groups, and breakout rooms has made this process so much easier. Any courses like this that often use small discussions are great online.
17) I think all classes are better in-person. However, the more substantive the content, the more online teaching is difficult.
18) Too broad a Q
19) Doctrinal courses work best and experiential learning and workshops are most difficult.
20) doctrinal courses are amenable to online as are lectures that are not interactive
21) electives
22) most

More than 80

1) Electives most, 1L least
2) small upper level electives
3) Doctrinal courses are very amenable to online learning. Clinics and skills training classes present special challenges.
4) Upper division electives and writing courses
5) Least amenable are legal research, criminal and civil clinical work, and trial and appellate advocacy classes. All ordinary substantive content courses are fine for online teaching.
6) Most any class can be taught online and taught well. The problem is that the instructor has to put a great deal of time in preparing the class to go online even if she has taught the subject many times before. They are, in many ways, two, different classes. Covid forced us all online and many of us found that frustrating.
7) I don't know. Skills classes are difficult online, doctrine is a little easier.
8) Legal Reasoning Advanced Legal Analysis
9) all of them
10) least: clinics; simulated course like interviewing, counseling, negotiation; trial techniques most: straight lectures
11) Upper class most, clinical least
12) Least: Clinics and skills courses Most: "Law and... [economics, sociology, whatever]
13) Most: those with simple fact patterns (e.g. basic torts) Least: those with more complex fact patterns (e.g. secured trans, negotiable instruments, MandA
14) Interestingly, I have found that that live client clinic is working on a remote format provided it is live. Because our clients are experiencing domestic and intimate partner violence we are able to keep them safe in this remote

format. Our hearing are all by zoom, as are our client meetings. Because we have a small group of students in the clinic zoom is working very well, In fact, we meet much more often given the convenience of last minute scheduling with zoom. It is better because we can see each other and pull up work. As compared to the emergency calls we use to schedule for matters that arose ore-Covid. As for the doctrinal classes I teach such as Evidence, Ethics, Family Law and others, I have concerns that some students may not be paying attention given the larger size of those classes.

15) Not sure
16) On line learning only works with less than 10 students in the class. Any larger and meaningful participation by the students is compromised. THe larger the class the more it becomes a lecture on line.
17) Most: tax and other technical subjects in which students are expected to find specific answers Least: first year courses, in which I expect few online students "get" the course objectives
18) Don't know
19) Law school classes should be in person. There is very little about law school that is amenable to online instruction.
20) Large first year classes (such as Contracts, torts, etc.) because you can easily split students into small groups. This is very powerful -- possibly the best thing about online teaching.

What new programs or courses do you think the law school has or may now be able to develop now that faculty is more familiar with distance education? Broken out by law school ranking

Top 20

1) Executive education
2) More short subject lunch presentations over Zoom and recorded content.
3) Greater variety of courses and content
4) more graduate courses and executive courses for international students
5) "Executive" courses for distance learners
6) None
7) Online degrees
8) Much easier to get guest speakers if they're online
9) Not sure
10) More remote guests and conference type panels

21-45

1) None
2) n/a
3) More flexible JD and non-JD programs that allow for a split of in-person and online learning.
4) Use of virtual platforms for presenting and making arguments or branding efforts.
5) I don't know yet.
6) n/a
7) Remote tech applied to legal endeavors. for example, I expect court proceedings to continue with heavy remote appearances. Learn and teach how to use tech effectively in such settings.
8) N/A
9) Technology in the Law
10) Every law school will be trying to capture revenue via distance learning. Consequently, very few of them will succeed.
11) An ADR Track. More access to more resources.
12) N/a
13) unlimited
14) They have already decided to do an integrated evening program that allows up to a certain percentage of attendance virtually.

46-80

1) ?
2) We will be moving our evening JD division increasingly online.
3) non-degree on-line certificate courses
4) Clinical courses
5) Cross-listed with other schools in the university
6) International offerings
7) Certificate instruction for practicing lawyers or other professionals.
8) I hope that the law school can better leverage distance education to facilitate students working or completing externships in other cities.
9) don't know
10) Some additional online classes from remote adjuncts
11) allows to join in experts who are in other states, traveling students, minimizes commuting times etc
12) NA
13) Mini-seminars
14) More specialized courses taught to multiple law schools
15) more specialized electives

More than 80

1) My school has no intention to do any of this, bc our administration does not seem to understand its value
2) shift the part-time program to significantly online
3) Programs relying on outside speakers--it is much easier to get experts to pop in on Zoom than it is in-person. I could see putting an entire course together based on guest appearances by people with expertise. For example, in my innocence clinic, I can have exonerees and their lawyers present to class frequently, based on issues in their cases, from all over the country.
4) Provide law-related education to non-lawyers
5) I don't think the school is interested in using online education to develop new programs or courses.
6) We have a sizeable number of international students. Much more of that instruction will happen online. This should reduce costs once the courses have been taught several times.
7) Using the technology for symposia so that speakers from all over can present.
8) specialty courses with low enrollment
9) graduate programs taught both in person and online
10) We should run away from online like it's on fire
11) Smaller skills classes would be a great area to focus on. Bringing in practitioners who would be more willing to jump on to Zoom from their offices for an hour to work with students would, in my opinion, work very well.
12) Better supplemental lectures

13) I do not understand this question
14) Don't know

Table 11.1 What percentage of law school classes do you feel should remain predominantly online post pandemic?

	Mean	Median	Minimum	Maximum
Entire sample	17.48	15.00	0.00	100.00

Table 11.2 What percentage of law school classes do you feel should remain predominantly online post pandemic? Broken out by law school ranking

Law school ranking	Mean	Median	Minimum	Maximum
Top 20	17.73	10.00	0.00	100.00
21-45	13.15	10.00	0.00	50.00
46-80	19.80	20.00	0.00	50.00
More than 80	20.47	16.25	0.00	50.00

Table 11.3 What percentage of law school classes do you feel should remain predominantly online post pandemic? Broken out by title of respondent

Title of respondent	Mean	Median	Minimum	Maximum
Professor	14.36	15.00	0.00	50.00
Assistant/Associate Professor/Lecturer or Research Fellow	29.71	15.00	0.00	100.00
Adjunct/Clinical Faculty	18.75	17.50	0.00	50.00
Emeritus	32.50	32.50	15.00	50.00
Other	12.50	5.00	0.00	37.50

Table 11.4 What percentage of law school classes do you feel should remain predominantly online post pandemic? Broken out by age of respondent

Age of respondent	Mean	Median	Minimum	Maximum
44 or under	30.31	20.00	0.00	100.00
45-54	16.18	12.50	0.00	50.00
55-65	15.94	15.00	0.00	50.00
Over 65	15.68	15.00	0.00	50.00

Table 11.5 What percentage of law school classes do you feel should remain predominantly online post pandemic? Broken out by gender of respondent

Gender of respondent	Mean	Median	Minimum	Maximum
Male	13.11	10.00	0.00	50.00
Female	26.58	20.00	0.00	100.00

Table 11.6 What percentage of law school classes do you feel should remain predominantly online post pandemic? Broken out by law school student enrollment

Law school student enrollment	Mean	Median	Minimum	Maximum
Less than 400	21.25	15.00	0.00	50.00
400 - 500	17.40	16.25	0.00	50.00
501 - 750	13.91	15.00	0.00	50.00
More than 750	19.50	15.00	0.00	100.00

Table 11.7 What percentage of law school classes do you feel should remain predominantly online post pandemic? Broken out by public or private status

Public or private status	Mean	Median	Minimum	Maximum
Public	21.17	18.75	0.00	50.00
Private	14.67	10.00	0.00	100.00

Table 11.8 What percentage of law school classes do you feel should remain predominantly online post pandemic? Broken out by number of courses taught in the past semester

Number of courses taught in the past semester	Mean	Median	Minimum	Maximum
None	17.00	15.00	0.00	50.00
One	14.86	15.00	0.00	50.00
Two	21.44	15.00	0.00	100.00
More than Two	16.05	18.75	0.00	33.00

What practices that developed during the pandemic do you feel should be held over and extended post pandemic? Broken out by law school ranking

Top 20

1) Offering virtual office hours and student services.
2) Virtual office hours can work well, as can some class components.
3) Optional remote learning
4) Students and faculty should be able to choose to hold office hours/supervision online for greater convenience and to allow more accessibility of faculty for students. Otherwise, all classroom teaching should return 'live'.
5) Automatic class recording; offering the possibility of Zoom for a variety of purposes
6) Greater flexibility
7) Zoom office hours
8) Heavy use of powerpoints; smaller classes
9) Ability to conduct some sessions by Zoom and to conduct some meetings online
10) Workshops and conferences on-line rather than in person
11) Use if zoom technology for breakout sessions or smaller meetings
12) More online interaction
13) Zoom classes work
14) Integration of remote guest visits, ability to teach remotely instead of rescheduling classes (for a limited number of classes)
15) Zoom availability for conferences and symposia
16) On line class option
17) Guest appearances by Zoom.
18) Hybrid teaching

21-45

1) Non
2) The ability to use Zoom in place of in-person makeups when the instructor cannot be present and for speakers who cannot travel to campus
3) More videoconferencing meetings, or the option of hybrid meetings in case students / employees cannot attend in person.
4) Quality online asynchronous learning--whether for an entire course or, more likely, portions of courses
5) Use of virtual platforms to groom skill sets for law students.

6) I would continue to offer as an alternative for interested students the option to have virtual appointments/office hours with faculty as it makes it easier and convenient to meet when an in-person component is unnecessary.
7) Having meetings over Zoom.
8) Zoom attendance. Lessons in tech for faculty and students.
9) Recording of classes
10) Use Zoom for make-up classes
11) Online academic conferences and guest lecturers.
12) Choice of students to take any class remotely.
13) Emergency plan for online teaching in future pandemics
14) None.
15) Online learning, care for students exhibited more clearly and often, technical help
16) Virtual office hours
17) More online courses.
18) Ongoing remote learning while bringing back in class teaching
19) Larger meetings over Zoom, Zoom office hours, recordings of classes made available for students who are sick
20) on-line course offerings or at least, the option
21) Options for virtual office hours, some class sessions.
22) Virtual office hours, options to attend virtually if can't make in person.
23) Sanitation
24) Expanded student access to materials and professors
25) Virtual attendance for conferences. Zoom has enable global participation in conferences.
26) Faculty workshops with visiting scholars presenting their work remotely.

46-80

1) Conferences should be on Zoom.
2) Effective use of online courses.
3) Zoom office meetings
4) Off line content, use of Canvas
5) Online office hours
6) Providing more online opportunities for faculty student interaction outside of class meetings
7) Limited remote instruction.
8) Remote office hours -- so much more convenient for students. Making content available on line. Allowing faculty to choose whether to teach remotely or in person.
9) online classes for those out of state or the area
10) Hybrid for snow days or sick students, some online courses

11) Allowing for Zoom attendance at meetings; incorporating more online and hybrid course options
12) Having online courses
13) In lecture based classes you don't miss much using zoom
14) Follow the science
15) Option to attend class via video
16) receptivity to on-line education for all students
17) The incorporation of technological tools to engage students
18) More online interaction, more lectures online, integrating more tech, doing in the moment research and projects.
19) Make virtual options available for students and faculty as occasional options when needed.
20) Extra lectures posted on Canvas
21) The flexibility to work from home.
22) Zoom faculty meetings and briefings. Online training.
23) Hyflex classes.
24) Certain meetings and speakers through zoom
25) Zoom was much better than any of us thought. In this day and age, I don't think we should ever go back to not using this tool

More than 80

1) Remote learning
2) Continued use of Zoom for meetings with students and others.
3) More flexible attendance policies that allow students and professors an online option for some classes. I plan to use a "blended campus" approach to all classes after things return to norma.
4) Faculty meetings online, committee meetings online, office hours online
5) Some social distancing. Availability and use of hand sanitizer. Minimal physical contact.
6) A great deal of student advising and student conferences can be done online. Also, oral arguments work quite well online. Given that many courts will probably stay online, this is a good skill to inculcate in our students.
7) Zoom availability.
8) The ability to teach classes virtually under extenuating circumstances.
9) reduce administrative meetings and have an online attendance option
10) scholarly talks delivered online
11) Internet support
12) I hope none
13) better ventilation
14) Use of technology

15) Zoom is a good platform for meetings, large events and some classroom teaching. This is in keeping with the practice of law. Lawyers are moving to remote client meetings which is more convenient for clients.
16) Supplementary material in video lectures
17) Use of web based intranets to publish materials to students to ease access to curriculum is critical.
18) Better testing options
19) The practice of using Zoom
20) Online learning
21) Flexibility in working from home.
22) Student options for virtual learning
23) Zoom office hours, student meetings, committee meetings
24) Online collaboration with students.
25) Recording classes so students can watch or rewatch later.
26) Online teaching

www.ingramcontent.com/pod-product-compliance
Ingram Content Group UK Ltd.
Pitfield, Milton Keynes, MK11 3LW, UK
UKHW051241300926
15471UKWH00015B/1484